★Abraham Lincoln★

Americans of Character

Elizabeth Kay

Young People's Press
San Diego

JB
LINCOLN

About the *"Six Pillars of Character"*

Each section of this book includes a drawing of a pillar.

Above each pillar is a word. These words—six in all—name

the most important traits that a person of good character

has. Together, these words are known as the *"Six Pillars of*

Character." On pages 22 – 27 you will be exploring what

these pillars mean.

Copyright © 1997 by Young People's Press, Inc.
"The Character Education Publisher" ™

Cover photo courtesy of Illinois State Historical Library.

Published in the United States of America.

2 3 4 5 6 7 8 9 - 02 01 00 99 98 97
ISBN 1-57279-060-1

Table of Contents

1 HAT

Abraham Lincoln wore a tall, black hat. It protected him from rain and kept him warm. Sometimes he carried his mail in it! But under that hat, there was a man who knew right from wrong. He saw slavery and hated it. Later, he signed a law that freed the slaves.

Abraham Lincoln stood up for his beliefs.

TRUSTWORTHINESS

2 PENNIES

As a young man, Abraham Lincoln worked in a store in New Salem, Illinois. One time, he accidentally charged a woman too much money. It doesn't matter exactly how

TRUSTWORTHINESS

much money it was—some say two pennies. Lincoln
walked a long way just to give her the pennies back.
Actions like these earned him the nickname Honest Abe.

**Abraham
Lincoln told
the truth.**

3 SARAHS

Sarah Lincoln was Abraham's older sister. When their mother, Nancy Hanks Lincoln, died, their new stepmother was named Sarah Bush Lincoln. She already had a daughter who was also named Sarah. That made three people named Sarah living in a one-room log cabin! Do you think it was confusing? In the crowded log cabin, Lincoln was courteous. He appreciated his family, and they all loved him.

RESPECT FOR OTHERS

Sarah Bush Lincoln
(the only one of the three
Sarahs ever photographed)

**Abraham Lincoln was
considerate of others.**

4 CHILDREN

Abraham Lincoln and his wife, Mary, had four children. They were all boys. Lincoln loved them very much, and he always showed it. Once, Willie and Tad burst into an important meeting to ask their father to pardon their

CARING

soldier doll, Jack, who had fallen asleep on sentry duty.

Before he returned to his meeting, Lincoln wrote:

The Doll Jack is pardoned, by order of the President. A. Lincoln

Abraham and Mary Todd Lincoln, with three of their sons—Willie, Robert, and Tad

Abraham Lincoln was kind.

5 YEARS

Abraham Lincoln was President of the United States for five years. The people of the United States voted for him because they believed that he could be trusted to keep the Union together. They were right. He freed the slaves, led the Union Army, and cared about the southern states. He was shot and killed in the fifth year of his presidency.

TRUSTWORTHINESS

Abraham Lincoln, 1861

Abraham Lincoln, 1865

Abraham Lincoln was trustworthy.

6 MOVES

Abraham Lincoln moved many times in his youth. He lived the same hard life of all settlers on the prairie. He grew to be big and strong by felling trees, building log cabins, carrying water from the creek, and always being helpful. He knew the good that comes from hard work: **"I am always for the man who wishes to work."**

Abraham Lincoln worked hard.

RESPONSIBILITY

MISSOURI TERRITORY

TAKE
BY JO

ILLINOIS
TERRITORY

Chicago

LAKE
LAKE ERIE

Illinois River

Salem
1831

Decatur
1830

Springfield
1837

Sangamon River

Wabash River

INDIANA
TERRITORY

OHIO

Little Pigeon Creek
1816

Anderson Creek

Ohio River

VIR

Mississippi River

Knob Creek
1811

Nolin Creek
1809

KENTUCKY

M A MAP
RY, 1825

TENNES

NORTH C

11

7 LETTERS

When Abraham learned to write his name, he wrote it over and over again—seven letters in his first name and seven in his last. He wanted to go to school, but he and his sister Sarah could only attend *if* there was a teacher and *if* they were not needed at home. So Lincoln had

Abraham Lincoln loved knowledge and always tried his best to gain it.

RESPONSIBILITY

to go to school "by littles." He always wanted to learn more. He borrowed books and read them many times. He loved words and practiced giving speeches to anyone who would listen.

8TH JUDICIAL CIRCUIT

In 1837 Abraham Lincoln became a lawyer in Springfield, Illinois. Part of his job was to help people who had legal problems no matter how far away they lived. This meant that he rode "the Circuit" from town to town in a buggy or on horseback. Often he was circuit riding for weeks

> **Abraham Lincoln was a good friend to others.**

CARING

and even months! While he was away from home, he met many people who became his friends. They liked his honesty and the funny stories that he told so well. And he appreciated having friends: **"The better part of one's life consists of his friendships."**

9 TALL MEN

"The Long Nine" was the nickname given to the nine tall legislators from Sangamon County in 1836. They averaged six feet tall, but Lincoln was the tallest. All nine belonged to a political party called the Whigs. With Lincoln leading the way, they were successful in getting the Illinois state capital moved from Vandalia to Springfield. This made the people of Springfield happy—and it also made Lincoln even more popular. But Lincoln worked to keep people's trust and respect. Years later, when folks suggested that Lincoln run for president, he said yes.

Abraham Lincoln was a reliable leader.

Ninian W. Edwards

Job Fletcher

William F. Elkins

Robert L. Wilson

Abraham Lincoln

John Dawson

No photographs could be found of Andrew McCormick and Dan Stone, the other two members of "The Long Nine."

RESPONSIBILITY

Archer G. Herndon

10 APRIL 1865

When the long War Between the States was finally over, people wanted to celebrate. Some came to the White House and sang to President Lincoln. Abraham stepped outside and smiled. He said, **"I see you have a band with you. . . I have always thought 'Dixie' one of the best tunes I ever heard. . . I now request the band to favor me with its performance."** Since this was the special song of the Confederacy, some people hesitated to sing it. But in this way, Lincoln was already hoping to reunite the country.

FAIRNESS

Abraham Lincoln was fair to all people.

SUMMARY

Abraham Lincoln was born on February 12, 1809. He died on April 15, 1865. Most people remember Lincoln as the 16th President of the United States, but he was also a loving family member and a good friend. He was trustworthy, honest, considerate, and kind. Abraham Lincoln could be relied on to stand up for his beliefs, to be fair, to try his best, and to protect his friends, family, and country.

CITIZENSHIP

Abraham Lincoln was an
American of character.

The "Six Pillars of Character"

Look for the Trustworthiness pillar on the pages about Abraham Lincoln. Write what you think trustworthiness means. Some ideas are given below.

Be your best self.

TRUSTWORTHINESS

Tell the truth.

Keep your word.

Stand up for your beliefs.

Stand by your family, friends, and country.

Look for the Respect for Others pillar on the pages about Abraham Lincoln. Write what you think respect for others means. Some ideas are given below.

RESPECT FOR OTHERS

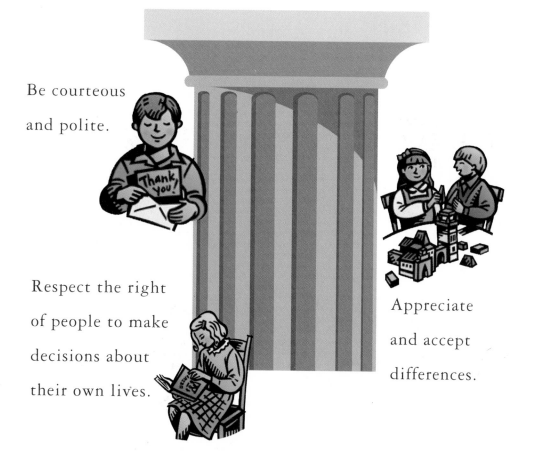

Be courteous and polite.

Respect the right of people to make decisions about their own lives.

Appreciate and accept differences.

Look for the Responsibility pillar on the pages about Abraham Lincoln. Write what you think **responsibility** means. Some ideas are given below.

Think before you act.

RESPONSIBILITY

Be reliable.

Do your best and keep trying.

Set a good example.

Look for the Fairness pillar on the pages about Abraham Lincoln. Write what you think fairness means. Some ideas are given below.

FAIRNESS

Treat all people fairly.

Listen to others.

Try to understand what others are saying and feeling.

Look for the Caring pillar on the pages about Abraham Lincoln. Write what you think caring means. Some ideas are given below.

CARING

Treat others like you want to be treated.

Help others.

Show you care about others through kindness, caring, and sharing.

Look for the Citizenship pillar on the pages about
Abraham Lincoln. Write what you think citizenship
means. Some ideas are given below.

CITIZENSHIP

Obey laws.

Do your share.

Respect
authority.

Protect the
environment.

Volunteer.

Acknowledgments

The author wishes to express her special thanks to Thomas F. Schwartz, State Historian of Illinois; and Kim Bauer, of the Illinois State Historical Society, for sharing the wealth of the Lincoln Collection, Springfield, Illinois.

The publisher gratefully acknowledges permission to use the following photographs:

Page i, 2, 5 (inset), 6-7, 9 (both), 11, 13, 14-15, 17 (all), 19 (inset), Courtesy of Illinois State Historical Library; 4-5, Keystone View Co./FPG; 20, © Peter Gridley/FPG; 21, © Telegraph Colour Library/FPG.

All illustrations pages ii, iii, 1-19, 28 by John Edens/Creative Freelancers. Illustrations pages 22-27 by Tracy Sabin.